RAS RODY
Organics
SIPS, BITES, & SWEETS

SPECIAL THANKS TO ROADSIDE FOOD PROJECTS

Photographs by Gabrielle Lurie

> *"The stone that the builder*
> *Refused shall become*
> *The head corner stone"*
>
> —ROBERT NESTA MARLEY

I WAS BORN ON APRIL 19, 1960 in the district of New Works in the parish of Westmoreland. My mom and dad were domestic farmers by which they raised seventeen children. I was the only begotten of both mom and dad therefore all I had were half brothers and sisters. Even though they were not married, my parents managed to support all seventeen children by planting crops and growing livestock. Far in the hills of southwest Jamaica, the air was always fresh and clean and at nights you could almost touch the stars. Mom led us as we sang together, she taught us to read the Bible and other interesting books, sometimes she told us duppy stories and African tales.

As kids, our dad worked us hard but we were always well fed. Dad spent all his days at the farm. He woke at five every morning to go tend to the fields producing a great variety of crops. He grew cane to sell to the West Indies Sugar Company. Times changed in the 1970's when farmers were introduced to pesticides and fertilizers. Before this happened, dad gave his plants natural organic manure, such as burnt cane, kitchen waste, and cow dung. His crops were always successful and the fruits and vegetables always tasted sweet. When he started using the bad chemicals, his crops yielded less, the food lost its taste, and the land dried out faster as he had to rework the same tired soil.

Even though his crops were failing, dad always managed to provide food for the house. But when we grew up, there was a significant change in our diets. We moved away from fresh fruits and vegetables towards the preserved and processed food available in the supermarket. He especially loved pork and passed this tradition onto my siblings. He would butcher a pig, give some to the village people and the rest he salted and left for us at home. All the other kids were fine eating pork but I was not created to be a meat eater. At age thirteen, I became very sick. On a December night, I was at home when all of a sudden a cold shivering and trembling came upon me. My whole body was swollen and I could taste death. Dad looked at me and his eyes filled with tears. He jumped up and told mom that they must get me to the doctor at once.

The nearest doctor was ten miles away. We had no transportation so dad saddled his mule and put me on its back. He and mom walked with me through the rugged hillside to the doctor. On my arrival, the doctor was surprised that I was still alive as my blood pressure was dangerously high. He admitted me to the Black River Hospital where I stayed for two months on total bed rest. With the good help of prayer, the care of the nurses and the doctor, and the support of my parents, I was able to recover. The first thing I ate after two months was plain vegetables; no grease, no dairy, nothing unnatural. What I learned about life at that young age was that one must be ready for changes and adjustments. For me, this was a change in my diet away from all meat products. My body could not sustain the high fat and sugar diet that was left with the colonial legacy in Jamaica.

My whole world changed. My mind was focused on a more righteous course. Love was growing inside me for everything around me: the plants, the animals, the people. With this new birth as a Rasta, I started to love growing and eating vegetables as a steward of the Earth. I never forgot that unhealthy eating had nearly taken my life, a powerful memory that precipitated this change in my diet. I have been a vegetarian for thirty years now and the steadfast loyalty to my own body pays me everyday. In my mystic life tradition, I learned that what we eat and drink determines our physical and spiritual conditions. But even when I gathered such great wisdom, the situation among the Jamaican people was unchanging.

I went back to the mountains in 1979 to show the people what I had discovered. It was not an easy road back in the high country. I went from being a young church boy fed pork to a Rastaman adorned in dreadlocks eating only vegetables. I moved to the remote mountains to continue my quest for a new way of life. The church and state waged war against the Rasta culture. With all the fight, I never stopped praying that one day people could see the vision that Rastafarian has to offer to the world. As time passed and my new life story began to manifest itself, I discovered that I could return to the lower village to live among the people. I would trod with the most humble appearance; some people would smile and some would frown.

In 1982, I left the mountains and returned to Negril. Still on the quest for a healthier lifestyle and with the memories of my late father, I researched with renewed enthusiasm how I could most honestly pursue my concept of life. I wanted to open my mind, body, and soul to the great universe and log onto the Earth's functioning system so I could find a solution to some of our fundamental weaknesses. We must not forget that it is the same elements that sustain all of us. People for too long have disregarded their own universe going up in flames by their own ignition.

There are nations whose culture is to raid the Earth's resources, there are other nations who want to serve Mother Nature in her purest form. There will be nation against nation. We as Rastafarian do not take path in the council of ungodly people, and we shall not be seated in the seat of scornful, we shall be as the tree planted so our fruits shall be a benediction to the Earth and its inhabitants. We do not render judgment or impose our system but rather serve as a model to those who yearn to be informed. A new beginning must start with organic living. This natural way of life takes nothing from nature. This mentality forges new connections between the Earth and its people.

If you take the West End Road in Negril just before the lighthouse, you will come upon Ras Rody Organic Food Store. I have been in operation for nearly fifteen years and people of all races and creeds eat at my roadside stand. There, my children and I demonstrate to people the importance of organic living. We prepare SIPS, BITES, and SWEETS, the three chapter titles in this cookbook. I dedicate each chapter to a tenet of a new organic lifestyle. SIPS demonstrates the value of slow food, as day-long preparations and shared meals strengthen community. Seasonality is at the center of BITES. The ackee, a staple of many of my savory preparations, serves as a prime example as the fruit only bears when it is safe to eat. This natural wonder begins to explain my great respect for the Earth's cycles. As the finale to a meal, SWEETS celebrates healthy satisfaction and nourished bodies. This book is manifesto for slow food, seasonality, and healthy satisfaction.

Organic living is not only eating and drinking right but beginning to adapt a different approach to everything in the course of daily life. People from the cities should find time to venture out and find land in the country where they can touch Mother Earth, where they can see the sun rise and the stars shine. This will open their eyes to the beautiful world that exists beyond the bustle of the big city. Eating right will set up a standard from which people can learn how the great universe runs, shedding light on new ways to heal Mother Nature and her children and bring them back to their former glory.

Organic living is the only way to save Mother Earth and its inhabitants. Plastics, factories, and vehicles as part of the industrial food chain all add up to this great pollution that threatens the ozone layer— the source of this Earth crisis. We as a people must discover the original way by which mankind lived in harmony with the Earth. As a true Rasta, I pray for the youths of all nations to achieve peace with themselves and the people around them; looking at life a different way and adapting a new approach to the way we treat animals, plants, and people. This Earth is all we have and it will take love and understanding to preserve its sacred bounty.

This book will give each reader a piece of the solution, the recipes will bring your family joy and satisfaction. Organic living and local networks of exchange will bring back to the Earth its natural nutrients and ease our dependence on chemicals and fossil fuels that are at the core of the fast food world. We all want a world of free movements, across the distant seas there are precious souls to teach and there are brothers and sisters that yearn for the true way of life. No man will be free until everyone is free. We shall each set to free a captured spirit and uplift the downtrodden. And I firmly believe that nothing is more liberating than food. This menu for a new organic life will help chart the new beginning. Blessed journey.

SIPS / *Coconut*

THE FOUNDATION OF ORGANIC living is slow food. The first step towards a new organic lifestyle is leaving fast food restaurants and returning to your backyard gardens. Even if you live in the heart of a city, find community gardens to relearn this important craft.

This simple concept is going to change a whole lot about your lives. Not only will you reengage with nature, but you will begin to build community. If you do not grow great variety, you can always barter with your neighbors to expand your menu. If your harvest fails one season, you can always rely on your neighbors with the promise of reciprocity next season.

Backyard gardens will rejuvenate interdependent local networks that sustained us on this planet for most of time. And when you see the beautiful process from seed to fruit, you will want to take more time to appreciate your food. Cooking is my expression of this appreciation.

My food is cooked slowly especially in soups— my most famous dishes and the highlight of this chapter. Coconut is the most important ingredient as it enhances the creamy texture in my soups. You cannot cook fast with the coconut; you have to take time so that you can derive all of its protein. The longer the soup simmers, the more nutritional and community value the food develops.

When I spend the day collecting ingredients and cooking food, I interact with so many people along the way. I have a local network of people, local farmers and American tourists alike who share in my organic lifestyle. The shared meal is the essence of my stand. It provides an open space for discussion, a classroom for those yearning to discover a new organic lifestyle. Together, we eject the fastness. SIPS will slow you down to enjoy a refreshing fruit juice or savor a comforting vegetable sou**p**.

"Eating what you grow is going to be the survival to the 21st century. When we eat together and when we share together that gives us strength."

Ginger Beer

½ pound young ginger

¼ cup natural cane juice

1 gallon water

2 tablespoons lemon juice

Grate ginger on fine setting or pulse in blender with water

Strain through fine strainer

If you do not have fresh cane juice, dilute ¼ cup cane sugar into ¼ cup water over low flame; cool before adding to ginger

Add cane juice to ginger water and finish with fresh lemon juice

Serve over ice with minced ginger

Coconut and Mango Smoothie

2 large mangos, peeled and deseeded

½ cup coconut flesh

2 cup rich coconut milk

1½ cups ice

10 leaves mint

2 teaspoons natural cane sugar

2 teaspoons lime juice

Add first four ingredients to the blender

Blend until it reaches smooth and rich texture

Muddle sugar and mint together

Finish smoothie with mint sugar and fresh lime juice

Lentil Soup

- 1 cup green lentils
- 7 cups water
- 2 carrots
- 1/2 bulb celery root
- 3 cloves garlic
- 3 sprigs fresh oregano
- ¼ scotch bonnet pepper
- 1 teaspoon coconut oil or other vegetable oil

Place garlic in aluminum foil with coconut oil; roast in 275 degree oven for one hour or until it is soft and develops strong fragrance

Bring the coconut milk and water to boil in large pot

Cut the carrot and celery root into ½ inch dice

Add to boiling pot with lentils and roasted garlic

Bring to boil again and then let it simmer for up to three hours over low heat

Add picked oregano and minced scotch bonnet pepper just before serving

Serve with sweet festival bread

Banana and Papaya Smoothie

- 3 large ripe bananas
- 1 large papaya
- ½ cup soy milk
- 1½ cup water
- 1 cup cubed ice
- ½ cup oats
- 3 tablespoon honey
- ½ teaspoon nutmeg

Soak oats in water for 5 minutes

Add all the ingredients to the blender

Blend until it reaches rich texture

Serve chilled for breakfast

Pumpkin Soup

1 fresh pumpkin or 2 cups unsweetened pumpkin puree

2 cups coconut milk

5 cups water

2 potatoes, peeled

2 sprigs fresh thyme

6 leaves fresh sage

1 stick cinnamon bark

2 tablespoons olive oil

1 teaspoon black pepper

→

Cut the pumpkin in half, deseed and rub with coconut oil

Place thyme sprigs and sage on both halves and wrap in aluminum foil

Place over open flame or in 350 degree oven and roast until flesh is tender

Scoop flesh from the peel

Bring the coconut milk and water to boil in large pot

Add pumpkin and chopped potato to pot with boiling coconut milk

Let it simmer for up to three hours with one stick of cinnamon bark and fresh sage leaves

Puree in blender until smooth, finish with fresh olive oil and black pepper

Serve in calabash bowls with roasted almonds

Guava and Lime Juice

12 fresh guava

3 limes

6 cups water

1 teaspoon young ginger

10 leaves fresh basil

→

Puree guava and fresh ginger with water for 30 seconds

Adjust water to right consistency, juice should have smooth and light texture

Halve the limes and press with reamer to extract the juices

Add lime to guava juice and strain together through fine strainer

Add torn basil leaves with strained juice into pitcher; serve over crushed ice

BITES / *Ackee*

MY KITCHEN IS DIFFERENT than most kitchens. Lots of chefs go to the store to buy preserved and packaged food to write their menus. We try to do everything from scratch. All the raw material: we produce it, we provide it, we fix it. So our kitchen has a different touch of elegance and taste. We do not have to go to the supermarket; we hunt from the ground, from our farms, from the trees, from everything around us.

Our food is cast upon the Earth, it depends on the sun and the rain. If you visit a farm, you will see that everything takes time to grow. You cannot force it. If you take time to grow and prepare your food, you are going to have time to live right. When a seed is planted, that seed has to grow through many stages before it becomes edible. Nothing that Mother Nature gives us comes over night. This teaches us the way of nature.

We should try to eat with the natural cycles, never going above it to accommodate the demands of the fast food world. Fast food has no values. When I was young, we would raise our chickens for nearly a year before they were ready to eat. Now, the industrial farmers do not even wait six weeks. They inject the chickens with hormones and antibiotics to speed up the process. There is no respect for the natural cycles as prescribed by Mother Nature.

The ackee is a staple in many of the dishes in this chapter. Nothing more clearly illustrates the value of seasonality than ackee. Before the fruit opens up and reveals its black seed it is poisonous. But at the right moment as decided by Mother Nature the fruit bears and is safe to eat. This natural wonder informs the Rastafarian reverence for the Earth's cycles. BITES is a testament to my profound respect for the natural world.

"We didn't grow fast. In our lifetime, a year takes long to come. Slow life. Slow food, that's what I make."

Rice and Pees

1 cup brown rice

1 cup red peas

2 cups water

1 cup coconut milk

2 sprigs thyme

2 cloves garlic

→

Soak the red peas overnight in water

Cook the peas with coconut milk, water, minced garlic, and thyme for 1 hour

Stir the rice into the peas and bring to a boil

Cover and let simmer on low heat for 30 minutes

Remove from heat once water is absorbed and rice is tender

Rice and Pumpkin

1 cup brown rice

1 cup pumpkin

2 cups water

½ cup coconut milk

1 teaspoon all spice

1 stick cinnamon bark

→

Cut the pumpkin into ¼ inch dice

Add all the ingredients into pot and mix together

Bring to boil over high heat

Cover and let simmer for about 30 minutes

Remove from heat once water is absorbed and rice is tender

Sauteed Cabbage

2 cups cabbage

1 small onion

2 cloves garlic

2 teaspoons coconut oil

2 sprigs thyme

→

Shred cabbage on fine grater and slice onion and garlic

Place all three ingredients into hot pan with coconut oil

Sautee for 5 minutes until the cabbage begins to break down

Finish with fresh picked thyme

Steamed Callaloo

1 bundle callaloo

1 small onion

2 teaspoons coconut oil

½ teaspoon all spice

½ scotch bonnet pepper, deseeded

→

Rough cut callaloo and slice onion

Place all three ingredients into hot pan with coconut oil

Sautee together with allspice and sliced scotch bonnet pepper

Reduce heat to low and steam covered for 10 minutes until the callaloo is tender

Serve as side dish as a healthful addition to the meal

Red Pea Stew

2 cups red peas

2 cups coconut milk

2 cups water

2 potatoes

2 carrots

8 okra

2 tablespoons fresh ginger

3 sprigs fresh thyme

½ teaspoon all spice

→

Soak the red peas overnight

Cook the peas with coconut milk and water for 30 minutes

Dice the potatoes, carrots, and okra into ¼ inch cubes while the peas are cooking

Add diced vegetables and cook on low heat until stew is rich and creamy

Season with grated fresh ginger and allspice

Finish with picked thyme and serve warm over brown rice

Curried Vege Chunks

1 pound vege chunks or seitan

1 small onion

2 tablespoons fresh ginger

1 small celery root

2 carrots

2 teaspons fresh turmeric or 2 teaspoons curry powder

4 tablespoons coconut oil

1 cup coconut milk

½ cup water

→

Cook vege chunks in coconut milk and water over moderate heat for 15 minutes

Dice onion, carrots, and celery into ¼ inch cubes and grate the ginger into paste

Cook grated turmeric into coconut oil for 2 minutes to extract color

If using dried curry powder, do not add until after the vegetables are sautéed.

Add diced vegetables and sautee over moderate heat for 10 minutes

Add cooked vege chunks with its liquid and simmer for 30 minutes to let the turmeric flavor the entire dish, careful not to over reduce coconut milk

Serve with brown rice

Filling / *Ackee Patties:*

2 cups fresh ackee or 2 cans precooked ackee

4 cups water, only for fresh ackee

1 onion

½ teaspoon allspice

1 scotch bonnet pepper

2 tablespoons coconut oil

→ If using fresh ackee, boil in water for 20 minutes and strain
Dice the onions and sautee in coconut oil for 5 minutes
Add the ackee, halved scotch bonnet pepper, and allspice
Cook together for another 10 minutes on moderate heat
Remove the pan and let the filling cool while preparing the dough

Roasted Pepper:

3 sweet peppers

3 stalks scallion

1 scotch bonnet pepper

2 tablespoons coconut oil

5 leaves fresh basil

→ Rub peppers and scallions with oil and roast over open flame or on grill until charred

Allow to cool in covered container, allowing the peppers to steam to help with peeling

Peel and dessed the pepper, slice the peppers and scallions

Toss together with torn fresh basil leaves and it let cool while making the dough

Pattie Dough:

4 cups bread flour

2 teaspoons baking powder

½ cup vegetable oil

1 cup water

½ teaspoon sugar

→ Mix flour and baking powder in a large mixing bowl

Add water slowly and combine with fingers to right consistency

Cut dough into 8 equal portions

Roll into 1/8 inch thick flat rounds on floured surface

Add filling into the center of the rolled dough and fold end to end to form half circles

Be careful to enclose all the filling and remove all air from within the cavity

Crimp the edges with a fork and cut for clean edge

COOKING:

1 cup coconut oil

Heat pan with coconut oil

Fry patties on both sides until dough is cooked and rich golden brown color

Serve with pickled scotch bonnet peppers

Pickled Scotch Bonnet Peppers / Homemade Pickapep

20 scotch bonnet peppers

½ cup natural cane juice

1 cup apple cider vinegar

½ cup water

¼ cup pimento berries

2 teaspons fresh ginger, sliced

2 sprigs thyme

1 sterilized canning jar

→

Boil the scotch bonnet peppers in water for 10 minutes to temper its heat; strain

Warm all the pickling ingredients together in separate pot until it reaches a boil

Pour the warmed mixture over the peppers and place into sterilized jar

Seal and allow to pickle in cool place for at least 1 week

Okra and Tomato Stew

12 large okras

3 ripe tomatoes, peeled and deseeded or 1 cup whole peeled tomatoes

½ onion

2 cloves garlic

1 teaspoon pimento berries

10 leaves fresh basil

2 tablespoons coconut oil

→

Cut the okra into ¼ rounds and slice the onion and garlic

Sautee onion, garlic, and okra in coconut oil over moderate heat

Add chopped tomatoes and crushed pimento berries after ten minutes

Stir together and let it stew together over low heat for 30 minutes

Finish with torn basil leaves and serve with corn meal fritters

Fried Okras

20 large okras, quartered

1 cup flour, fine ground preferred

2 tablespoons corn starch

2 teaspoons baking powder

1¼ cups sparkling water

5 leaves fresh basil

→ Mix flour, corn starch, and baking powder together

Whisk in water until it is a smooth and light batter

Drench okras and fresh basil in batter, careful to remove any excess

Fry in two batches in 350 degree oil until golden brown and crispy

Drain on towels to remove excess oil

Squeeze fresh lime juice on fried okras just before serving

Watercress Salad

2 cups fresh watercress leaves, picked and cleaned

½ cup heart of palm

4 tablespoons coconut oil

2 tablespoons lime juice

½ teaspoon acacia honey

½ teaspoon coriander seed

→ Rough cut callaloo and slice onion

Place all three ingredients into hot pan with coconut oil

Sautee together with allspice and sliced scotch bonnet pepper

Reduce heat to low and steam covered for 10 minutes until the callaloo is tender

Serve as side dish as a healthful addition to the meal

Roasted Breadfruit

1 breadfuit

→ Roast whole breadfruit over open fire on all sides, up to 1 hour

Peel or scrape charred skin and serve with stews

SWEETS / *Sugar Cane*

OUR SWEETS ALL BEGIN with natural sugars. As a child growing up, I always chewed on a fresh piece of sugar cane when I wanted sweets. I want to remind you that the supermarket can be dangerous. Lots of people today have diabetes, have high blood pressure, have lots of different ailments; it is the processed sugars from the supermarket stored in them for a long time.

We should not trust the big corporations to feed us. As long as I live in my cane fields, how can I face their judgment? The processed foods in the supermarket are loaded with corn sweeteners that have caused soaring obesity among my fellow Jamaicans.

All the sweets in this chapter use natural cane sugar. I did not discover my real diet until I was eighteen years old and found Rastafarian culture. That is when I learned that organic eating is the true way; it was the only way my body was not going to get stocked up with the toxins that had nearly taken my life as a young boy.

Food was the introduction to my new lifestyle. Had I not eaten this way, I would not be here talking to you today. Food was a basic part of my survival. Everything you eat is going to build or break your health. That is why I say let your food be your medicine…I use every ingredient for a reason. My philosophy is all about promoting good health.

I use every ingredient for a reason. The reason I cook this way is because I want to keep peoples bodies healthy. This food was developed to nourish bodies. Beyond the politics of organic living, the essence of this food is healthy satisfaction. This feature of thoughtful eating highlighted in SWEETS will transform a current trend into a lasting culture.

"Once you open your mind to something and you are true to yourself, that truth will lift you and you will go to higher places."

Fried Dumplings

1 cup bread flour

1/2 teaspoon baking powder

2 tablespoons dark brown sugar

1/2 cup cold water

2 cups coconut oil – warmed until it becomes liquid

Add the coconut oil to bread flour, baking powder, and brown sugar, mix

Pour in water and combine with fingers until it reaches soft texture

Roll firmly into 1" round balls in your hands, ensuring to work the dough

Allow 1 hour to proof the dough, allowing the baking powder to rise
Heat vegetable oil in heavy bottomed pot to 350 degrees F

Drop dumplings into the hot oil and fry until it reaches golden brown color

Serve with pineapple sauce

Pineapple Sauce

1 cup fresh pineapple juice

5 leaves fresh basil

2 teaspoons fresh lemon juice

Reduce pineapple juice until it develops into syrup, cool before serving

Just before serving, finish the sauce with torn basil leaves and fresh lemon juice

Banana and Corn Meal Festival

2 cups fine cornmeal

½ cup AP flour

2 teaspoons baking powder

½ cup dark brown sugar

3 ripe bananas - chopped

1 - 1 ½ cups water

→

Sift all dry ingredients into mixing bowl with chopped banana

Add water until it becomes light batter

Heat frying pan with a small amount of vegetable oil

Spoon 1/6 of batter into the pan

Reduce heat to low and cook until it starts to bubble and develops golden brown color at the edge. Flip and cook the other side

Repeat the process 6 times and serve with hot tea

Carrot Cake

3 cups AP flour

¾ cup dark brown sugar

2 teaspoons baking power

½ teaspoon baking soda

½ teaspoon all spice

½ teaspoon cinnamon

½ teaspoon salt

5 medium carrots

1 ripe banana

½ teaspoon fresh ginger

¾ cup vegetable oil

¾ cup coconut milk

→

Preheat oven to 350 degrees F

Sift the flour, baking power, baking soda, all spice, cinnamon, and salt into large mixing bowl

In another mixing bowl mash the banana

Add the sugar and oil to the banana and wisk until light

Grate carrots and ginger on fine grater and mix with the sugar mixture

Gently fold ½ of the dry ingredients into the bowl

Slowly incorporate coconut milk until it becomes light batter

Gently fold the rest of the dry ingredients into the bowl

Pour batter into greased cake dish and bake for 1 hour or until top browns

Cool before removing from the baking dish

Serve with caramel sauce

Coconut and Sage Caramel Sauce

½ cup coconut milk

½ cup coconut paste*

5 leaves fresh sage

½ cup brown sugar

→

Place sugar in dry heavy saucepan over moderate heat

Cook for about 10 minutes until the sugar begins to caramelize

Do not stir the sugar as it cooks, for this will cause it to crystalize

Once the sugar reaches a rich golden color, add the coconut milk and paste

Stir together with wooden spoon until mixture is smooth and coats the back of a spoon Remove from heat and steep with fresh sage

Serve over warm carrot cake

*To make the paste, work tender coconut flesh in mortar and pestle until smooth, if you can not make the paste, you can substitute an equal amount of coconut milk and cook the mixture a little longer

Coconut and Sweet Potato Pudding

3 cups sweet potatoes

2 cups AP flour

½ cup dark brown sugar

2 teaspoons baking power

½ teaspoon baking soda
½ teaspoon nutmeg

½ teaspoon cinnamon

1 cup rich coconut milk

2 teaspoons vanilla extract

→

Sift all dry ingredients into large mixing bowl

Grate sweet potatoes on fine grater and add to the dry ingredients

Slowly incorporate coconut milk until it becomes light batter

Stir in the vanilla extract

Pour the batter into greased and flowered 9x9 cake dish

Bake for 1 hour or until top browns

Cool before removing from the baking dish

Serve with coconut sauce

Coconut Sauce

1 cup coconut milk

1/2 cup dark brown sugar

¼ cup raisins

Nutmeg

→

Roughly chop raisins

In a heavy saucepan cook the coconut milk and sugar until the sugar dissolves and the sauce is thick enough to coat the back of a spoon - remove from heat

Add the raisins and a touch of freshly grated nutmeg

Serve warm

Ginger Beer Roasted Pineapple

1 ripe pineapple

24 oz ginger beer

1 bay laurel leaf

→

Cook the ginger beer with the bay leaf over medium high heat until it become a syrup

Preheat your oven to 375 degrees

Clean and peel the pineapple; cut into ½ inch cubes

Toss the chunks in enough syrup to lightly coat them – reserve some syrup for sauce

Place pineapple in a large baking pan

Roast at 375 degrees F until the pineapple is slightly brown

Coconut Roasted Bananas

6 bananas

1/3 cup dark brown sugar

½ cup coconut milk

¼ teaspoon grated nutmeg

→

Preheat your oven to 375 degrees F

Peel the bananas and place them in a 9x9 baking dish

Pour the coconut milk over the bananas

Sprinkle the sugar and grate the nutmeg on top of the bananas

Roast the bananas until they are slightly brown on top

Serve warm

Mango Jam

2 cups mango

1 cup sugar

1 cup water

1 tablespoon lime juice

¼ teaspoon dried chili flakes

→

Peel and chop the mango – discard the pit

Boil the mango in the water until tender

Add the sugar, lime juice, and chili flakes

Simmer until the mixture thickens

Cover and refrigerate

Pineapple Jam

2 cups pineapple

1 cup sugar

1 cup water

1 tablespoon lime juice

½ teaspoon grated ginger

→

Clean, peel, and finely chop the pineapple

Cook the chopped pineapple in the water until it is tender

Add the sugar, lime juice, and grated ginger

Simmer until the mixture thickens

Cover and refrigerate

Almond Milk Rice

1 cup brown rice

6 cups almond milk

½ teaspoon all spice

½ teaspoon salt

½ cup sugar

½ cup shredded coconut

½ teaspoon orange zest

½ teaspoon vanilla

½ cup slivered toasted almonds

→

Rinse the rice in water until the water runs clear

Combine rice and milk in a saucepan and bring to a boil stirring often

Reduce heat and add the spices and salt

Simmer until the rice is tender and creamy stirring often - this will take about 35 minutes

Remove from the heat – stir in the sugar, coconut, orange zest, and vanilla

Refrigerate until cool

Serve with slivered toasted almonds on top

I want to extend my deepest gratitude to everyone that has helped in the creation of this cookbook. The utmost thanks to HIS Imperial Majesty. Love and appreciation to my family for their constant support. Much respect to all the hard working people behind this book: Gabrielle Lurie, Sam West, Lea Howe, Michelle Wurth & Oliver Munday. Big up to all my friends throughout the years that have always stood by my side. Let this manifesto for healthy living be a guiding light as we chart the course ahead.

With humble regards,
Ras Rody 2011